SNAKES ALIVE

Anacondas

by Colleen Sexton

BLASTOFF!
3
READERS

BELLWETHER MEDIA • MINNEAPOLIS, MN

Note to Librarians, Teachers, and Parents:

Blastoff! Readers are carefully developed by literacy experts and combine standards-based content with developmentally appropriate text.

Level 1 provides the most support through repetition of high-frequency words, light text, predictable sentence patterns, and strong visual support.

Level 2 offers early readers a bit more challenge through varied simple sentences, increased text load, and less repetition of high-frequency words.

Level 3 advances early-fluent readers toward fluency through increased text and concept load, less reliance on visuals, longer sentences, and more literary language.

Level 4 builds reading stamina by providing more text per page, increased use of punctuation, greater variation in sentence patterns, and increasingly challenging vocabulary.

Level 5 encourages children to move from "learning to read" to "reading to learn" by providing even more text, varied writing styles, and less familiar topics.

Whichever book is right for your reader, Blastoff! Readers are the perfect books to build confidence and encourage a love of reading that will last a lifetime!

This edition first published in 2010 by Bellwether Media, Inc.

No part of this publication may be reproduced in whole or in part without written permission of the publisher. For information regarding permission, write to Bellwether Media, Inc., Attention: Permissions Department, 5357 Penn Avenue South, Minneapolis, MN 55419.

Library of Congress Cataloging-in-Publication Data

Sexton, Colleen.
Anacondas / by Colleen Sexton.
  p. cm. – (Blastoff! readers. Snakes alive!)
Summary: "Simple text and full-color photography introduce beginning readers to anacondas. Developed by literacy experts for students in kindergarten through third grade"–Provided by publisher.
Includes bibliographical references and index.
ISBN 978-1-60014-313-7 (hardcover : alk. paper)
1. Anaconda–Juvenile literature. I. Title.
QL666.O63S49 2010
597.96'7–dc22

2009037598

Text copyright © 2010 by Bellwether Media, Inc.
Printed in the United States of America, North Mankato, MN.

010110   1149

Contents

How Anacondas Look   4

Where Anacondas Live   10

Hunting and Feeding   14

Glossary   22

To Learn More   23

Index   24

Anacondas are the heaviest snakes in the world. There are four kinds of anacondas. The largest is the green anaconda.

Green anacondas can weigh more than 400 pounds (181 kilograms)! They can grow up to 30 feet (9 meters) long!

Anacondas are green, yellow, or brown. They have black spots. Their bellies are light yellow or cream-colored.

Dry, shiny **scales** cover their thick bodies. Each anaconda has a different pattern of scales under its tail.

scutes

Anacondas use the scales on
their bellies to move. These
large scales are called **scutes**.

The scutes grab on to the ground. Anacondas use strong muscles to pull on the scutes and move their bodies forward.

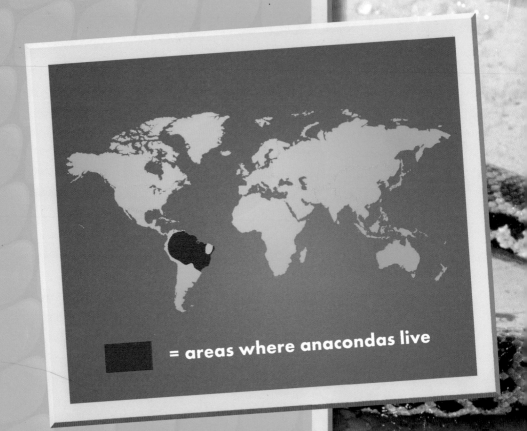

= areas where anacondas live

Anacondas live in the **tropical rain forests** of South America.

Anacondas need to control their body temperature. Sometimes they sun themselves to warm up.

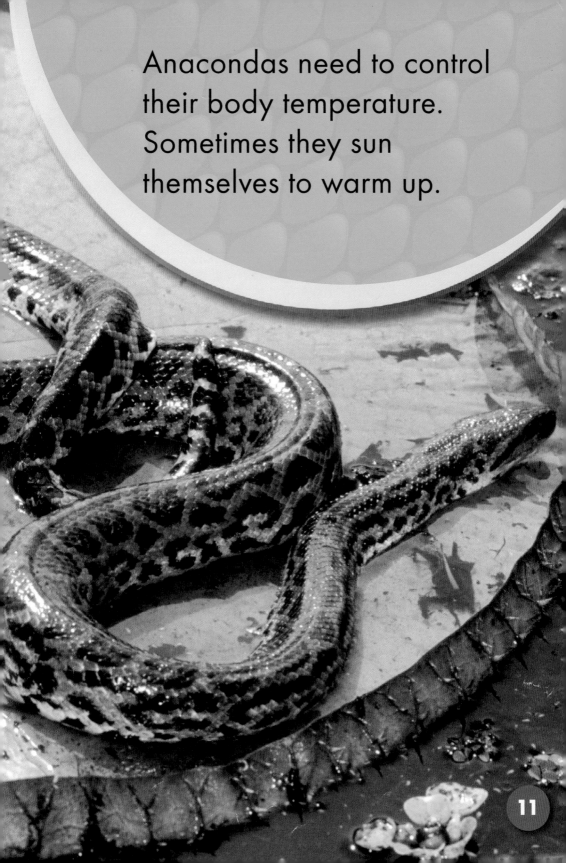

Anacondas cool off by resting in the mud by rivers and streams.

They slide into shallow water to hide. They poke the tops of their heads above water. Only their eyes and nostrils show.

Anacondas stay still in the water and wait for **prey** to come near. They stick out their forked tongues to pick up the scent of birds, deer, and **capybaras**.

Anacondas sneak up on their prey slowly. They quietly move closer and closer.

capybara

Anacondas quickly grab the prey with their sharp, curved teeth.

Anacondas wrap their strong bodies around prey and squeeze tighter and tighter. Soon the animals stop breathing and die.

Anacondas open their mouths wide to swallow the prey whole!

Their jaws come apart to let them stretch their mouths open even wider. Anacondas can swallow prey larger than their mouths.

Anacondas use muscles in their mouths to push the prey down their throats. It can take several hours to eat a large animal.

Anacondas rest for a long time after a big meal. They do not need to eat again for months!

Glossary

capybara—an animal that looks like a huge rat and lives in South America

prey—an animal hunted by another animal for food

scales—small plates of skin that cover and protect a snake's body

scutes—large scales on the belly of a snake that are attached to muscles; snakes use scutes to move from place to place.

tropical rain forest—a thick jungle with tall trees where a lot of rain falls; tropical rain forests are in hot areas of the world near the equator.

To Learn More

AT THE LIBRARY

Gibbons, Gail. *Snakes*. New York, N.Y.: Holiday House, 2007.

Gunzi, Christiane. *The Best Book of Snakes*. New York, N.Y.: Kingfisher, 2003.

Mattern, Joanne. *Anacondas*. Mankato, Minn.: Capstone Press, 2009.

ON THE WEB

Learning more about anacondas is as easy as 1, 2, 3.

1. Go to www.factsurfer.com.

2. Enter "anacondas" into the search box.

3. Click the "Surf" button and you will see a list of related Web sites.

With factsurfer.com, finding more information is just a click away.

Index

body temperature, 11

capybaras, 14, 15

color, 6

eyes, 13

forked tongues, 14

green anaconda, 4, 5

jaws, 19

length, 5

mouths, 18, 19, 20

muscles, 9, 20

nostrils, 13

prey, 14, 15, 16, 17, 18, 19, 20

scales, 7, 8

scutes, 8, 9

South America, 10

swallowing, 18, 19

teeth, 16

tropical rain forests, 10

The images in this book are reproduced through the courtesy of: blickwinkel / Alamy, front cover, p. 9; Morales, pp. 4 (small), 12; Jim Clare/npl /Minden Pictures, pp. 4-5; Frank Krahmer, pp. 6-7; Christophe Courteau/npl/Minden Pictures, p. 8; Jon Eppard, p. 10 (small); Berndt Fischer, pp. 10-11; Cooper/ Science Photo Library, p. 13; J & C Sohns, pp. 14-15; Juan Martinez, pp. 15 (small), 16 (small); Francois Gohier/Photo Researchers, Inc., pp. 16-17; Tony Crocetta/NHPA/Photoshot, p. 18; Erwin & Peggy Bauer/bciusa.com, p. 19; Francois Gohier/ardea.com, pp. 20-21.